3 1994 01014 3136

SANTA ANA PUBLIC LIBRARY

AR PTS: 2.0

D0459248

TIME TRAVELERS

ANCIENT
HORSEMEN
OF SIBERIA

Janet Buell

J 306.09573 BUE   SEP 0 9 1999
Buell, Janet
Ancient horsemen of
  Siberia
                        $23.40
CENTRAL   31994010143136

Twenty-First Century Books
Brookfield, Connecticut

Twenty-First Century Books
A Division of The Millbrook Press, Inc.
2 Old New Milford Rd.
Brookfield, Connecticut 06804

Text copyright © 1998 by Janet Buell
All rights reserved.

Library of Congress Cataloging-in-Publication Data
Buell, Janet
Ancient horsemen of Siberia / Janet Buell
p. cm. — (Time travelers)
Includes bibliographical references and index.
ISBN 0-7613-3005-4 (lib. bdg.)
1. Pazyryk culture. 2. Ethnology—Russia (Federation)—Altaĭskiĭ kraĭ. 3. Mounds—
Russia (Federation)—Altaĭskiĭ kraĭ. 4. Siberia (Russia)—Antiquities. 5. Horsemen and horse-
women—Russia (Federation)—Altaĭskiĭ kraĭ—History.   I. Title. II. Series.
GN780.2.P39B84 1998   98-9909
306'.0957'3—dc21   CIP
                                                                                             AC

Designed by Kelly Soong
Map by Jeffrey L. Ward

Printed in the United States of America
1   3   5   4   2

Photo Credits

Cover photograph courtesy of Sovfoto/Novosti.

Photographs courtesy of Sovfoto/Eastfoto: p. 8; Westlight/© Charles O'Rear: pp. 10, 13, 15, 17, 19, 22, 24, 26, 29, 31, 33, 47; Mjeda/Art Resource, N.Y.: pp. 36, 37, 46; Erich Lessing/Art Resource, N.Y.: p. 39; Gamma Liaison/© Bill Swersey: p. 44.

For Liz Tentarelli
boon companion, steadfast friend

ACKNOWLEDGMENTS

Many thanks to Jeanne Smoot for relating her experiences on the Ukok Plateau during the excavation of Ledi's kurgan. Thanks also to my editor, Pat Culleton, for seeing me through these first books.

C O N T E N T S

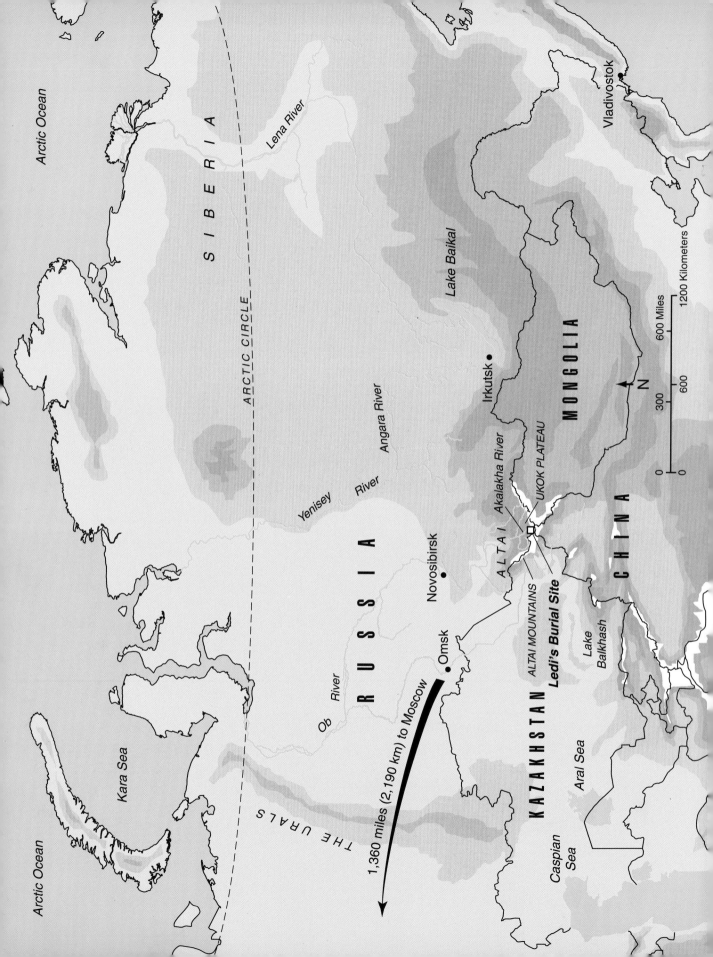

Arctic Ocean

S I B E R I A

Lena River

ARCTIC CIRCLE

Kara Sea

Arctic Ocean

Yenisey   River

Angara River

Lake Baikal

Vladivostok

Irkutsk

MONGOLIA

N

R U S S I A

Novosibirsk

Ob
River

Omsk

THE URALS

1,360 miles (2,190 km) to Moscow

Akalakha River

UKOK PLATEAU

A L T A I

ALTAI MOUNTAINS

Ledi's Burial Site

KAZAKHSTAN

C H I N A

Lake
Balkhash

Caspian
Sea

Aral Sea

300

600

1200 Kilometers

600 Miles

0

0

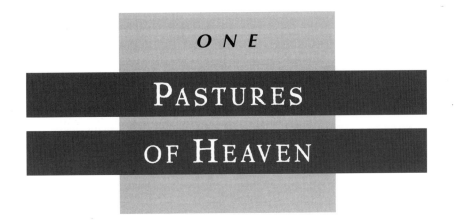

ONE

PASTURES

OF HEAVEN

Inside the little plywood hut, Russian archaeologist Natalya Polosmak pushed hard against the door. A storm had struck and drifts of snow now leaned heavily against the makeshift building. It was May 1993. Snow had trapped Polosmak and her team in their huts for hours. It didn't look good for the first day of the digging season in southern Siberia.

During three of the previous four years, the archaeologists had been excavating some of the ancient burial mounds, called kurgans, that lie scattered by the thousands across Siberia's high isolated plains. The kurgans and their artifacts are all that remain of an ancient culture called the Pazyryk, after the local word for burial mound. Historians know the Pazyryk were among the world's first horse riders. They lived some 2,500 years ago in the highlands of Siberia and buried their dead in kurgans, along with all the things they thought the dead would need in the afterlife.

By excavating kurgans, Polosmak hoped to find out more about these mysterious equestrians. She knew it wouldn't be easy. The Pazyryk constructed sturdy, elaborate mounds. And ancient thieves burrowed holes into many of them, hacking up corpses to get at the gold-covered jewelry they wore and making off with grave goods, all valuable clues to the Pazyryk way of life.[1]

THE END OF EVERYTHING

Since the Pazyryk left no written record of their lives, we don't know what they called the 7,500-foot-high plateau where Polosmak planned the dig. Modern residents call it the Ukok, which in their language means "the end of everything." Natives believe it offends the spirits to shout here, for the Ukok lies within the second layer of heaven, a place above ordinary life.

The Ukok Plateau does indeed seem to be out of the ordinary. The plateau is located in the Altai mountains, and the nearest city is a five-hour helicopter journey away. There are no cities or towns—only snow-capped mountains ring the high plateau. Very few people live here, and those who do gather their herds in summer and drive them to lower pastures. After they have gone, all that remains are grasslands that stretch for mile after lonely mile beneath a high blue dome of sky. [2]

Residents of the high plateau in the Altai mountains harvest hay when the weather permits.

8

The kurgan Polosmak intended to excavate was far beyond where the storm forced her to set up camp. Snow had made the mountain roads impassable, and the supply trucks could go no farther. Luck was with her, however. There was another kurgan within walking distance. Unfortunately, it had a collapsed center, which usually means the kurgan has been looted. Polosmak decided to excavate it anyway. There was always a chance she might find something worth retrieving.

ANCIENT WARRIORS

Three years earlier in 1990, during her first summer on the Ukok, Polosmak had excavated a Pazyryk tomb at a site not far from this one. Within the kurgan, she had found the skeletons of a forty-year-old man and a girl of about sixteen. The archaeological team had also found ten horses buried with them. The horses had been sacrificed so the two could ride in the afterlife. Archaeologists speculate the pair may have been father and daughter, or perhaps a man and his concubine, a secondary wife. Some historians believe the Pazyryk sacrificed a man's concubine so she, like the horses, could accompany him to the next world.

But the weaponry buried with the young woman—knives, bows, and battle-axes—hint at another relationship, that of a warrior and his young female battle page. Actually, the young woman may have been a warrior herself. The ancient Greeks wrote about warrior women who lived near the Black Sea. The women were part of an ancient culture called the Sarmatians. The Greeks called these women Amazons. Modern-day historians tell us the Sarmatians are culturally related to the Pazyryk.[3]

Polosmak knew archaeologists before her had excavated other Pazyryk kurgans throughout the region. The Russian anthropologist Sergei Rudenko was the most famous of these. Between the years 1925 and 1949 he dismantled five Pazyryk kurgans. Unfortunately, looters had gotten to all of them first, taking most of the burial offerings. But they didn't take everything. Tantalizing evidence of the Pazyryk survived the looting,

Archaeologists have discovered fifty ancient burial mounds near Pokrovka, Russia. Seven of those were female burials, which yielded daggers, swords, bronze arrowheads, and whetstones to sharpen weapons. Some scholars believe the weapons served a ceremonial purpose only. Forensic evidence shows they may be wrong. The leg bones of one thirteen- or fourteen-year-old girl show she spent a lifetime on horseback. A bent arrowhead in one of the women's bodies indicate she may have been killed in battle.

including the frozen, mummified remains of one of their chieftains in kurgan 2. The man, who died when he was about sixty years old, bore fantastic animal tattoos over his arms, chest, and lower legs. Though scientists aren't sure what significance the tattoos have, they do know he was probably a battle casualty. Two blows of a battle-ax killed him, and he had been scalped. His people recovered his body, and before they buried him, they tightly sewed another scalp onto his head with horsehair.[4]

Like most archaeologists interested in the Pazyryk, Polosmak hoped to make a significant discovery like Rudenko's. She began the short Siberian summer in 1993 armed only with hope and the makings of a temporary camp she and her team would call home for the next three months.

BEHIND THE SCENES

Archaeology is more than just spectacular finds of artifacts and human remains. It is hard work. In many cases, the sites that interest archaeologists are far from civilization. To complete the dig, scientists have to build camps where they live for its duration.

The archaeologists' campsite had a view of the Kazakhstan mountains in the distance.

Polosmak's group began by constructing huts from plywood the supply trucks brought. The archaeologists built lab huts where they and other scientists could study bodies or artifacts they found within the kurgan. They also built outhouses and tin-roofed sleeping huts. The sleeping huts had no running water and only one light bulb above the door. They were tiny, too—not more than 8 feet long on each side. Two bed shelves hung from the wall. Team members slept on these bed shelves, wrapped in sleeping bags or a cocoon of blankets to keep away the frigid night air. A large canvas tent served as their "mess tent," where they cooked and ate meals. Gasoline generators provided electricity for a few hours a day.[5]

A great deal of an archaeologist's work is what is called "grunt work." Grunt work gets its name from the grunts some people make when they pick up heavy objects. Archaeology is often full of grunt work like hauling rocks or shoveling dirt. Often students or volunteers labor beside the investigating archaeologist.

Excavating a kurgan takes a lot of grunt work because the Pazyryk went to great trouble to erect them, layering stones, rocks, boulders, and logs into deep holes. In these holes they had placed log burial chambers, very much like small log cabins, in which the Pazyryk laid the coffins of their dead. The Pazyryk constructed the top layer of Polosmak's kurgan with large stones laid out in a circular cap about a yard high. Grass eventually covered the kurgan as well. Polosmak's team removed the dirt and lugged rocks by hand. Six people labored for two weeks to clear hundreds of stones from the burial mound so they could start digging into the tomb.[6]

Digging Deeper

After they cleared the stones, the archaeologists discovered a hole dug into the burial mound that had been covered again. It meant looters had been here before them. The team didn't let their disappointment halt the work. They kept digging.

The next day, when they had gotten further into the kurgan, they came upon the skeletons of three horses. The horses lay on stones that served as a coffin lid. When the archaeologists lifted the stones, they found the skeleton of a man inside the coffin. Polosmak knew he was buried too shallowly to be a Pazyryk. The remains were those of a man from the Kora kobinsi culture, a group of people who often buried their dead inside Pazyryk kurgans. Unlike the Pazyryk, only modest grave goods accompanied the Kora kobinsi to the afterlife. All that remained of the man's worldly possessions were his three horses, their iron bits, two iron knives, animal bones, and a ceramic vessel.[7]

If the Pazyryk tomb below this grave was unlooted, Polosmak wondered why the robbers didn't dig further. Perhaps they didn't understand that another burial lay beneath this one. If they had paid close attention, they would have noticed a Pazyryk horse's head sticking up from a hole beneath the coffin. Now the archaeologists couldn't be sure exactly what awaited below. A renewed sense of hope electrified the team. As they continued to dig toward the lower burial, they grew more excited when they hit a frozen layer of dirt. Of all the kurgans excavated before, no one had ever discovered an unlooted, frozen tomb.

BAILING OUT

Workers sharpened their shovels to attack the frozen ground. Their target was the log burial chamber. After hours of digging, they came upon the bodies of horses, with skin and fur still clinging to their ancient bones. The horses lay against the wall of the log tomb. Then the team uncovered the best sign of all, the tomb's undamaged roof. As they stood there, the archaeologists understood just what this meant. The last people to look into this burial chamber were the Pazyryk, and that had been 2,500 years earlier.[8]

The team pried up the roof to reveal a frozen block of ice at the bottom of the tomb. Exposed to the warm sun, it quickly began to soften. Every morning the archaeologists bailed out the tomb, carrying away buckets of water and swatting the mosquitoes that pestered them relentlessly. The horses stank. It was slow, hard work.

Polosmak hoped that like many Pazyryk burials, the wooden tomb would contain more than one coffin. She probed the softening ice with an iron bar and dug through it until she could see dark shadows within. Then she ordered her team to speed up the melting process. Men brought water from a nearby pond and poured it into 55-gallon drums. They heated the drums with blow torches and used buckets to tote hot water to the ice. As they poured, others workers kept bailing the meltwater.[9]

As the ice melted around it, they could see the lid of an 8-foot-long coffin fashioned from a single log. It was so long Polosmak thought it might contain two people, since the Pazyryk were known to practice double burials. Leather cutouts in the shape of deer embellished the coffin's sides. Sturdy, 6-inch-long bronze nails secured the lid. Everyone waited eagerly as the nails were pulled out and the coffin lid came away.[10]

*This view of the log tomb shows the depth of the tomb
and a wooden coffin filled with ice.*

Inside the coffin lay a block of milky-white ice. It was what Polosmak had hoped for most. She knew scattered areas of permafrost, or permanently frozen subsoil, occur in some parts of Siberia. If she were lucky, water would have seeped into the coffin shortly after burial and then frozen there. If it had, there was a chance she would find more than just a skeleton. She might find a flesh-covered Pazyryk.

To keep tiny artifacts from washing away, archaeologists poured small cupfuls of hot water over the coffin ice. Other workers kept bailing. As they worked, the scientists considered the person or persons occupying the coffin. Who would it be? How much remained? What kind of death did he or she experience? Then, on the morning of July 19, something revealed itself from beneath the ice. It was a jawbone. And there was more—a cheekbone covered with remnants of flesh. Polosmak touched it lightly. Long ago this corpse had once been a living, breathing human being.

Later that afternoon, she uncovered the edge of a fur blanket below the corpse's jaw. Pulling it back revealed a flesh-covered shoulder bearing a tattoo of an elk. Its magnificent antlers spread like waves to their flower-tipped ends. Polosmak and the others couldn't believe their great luck. Forty-four years earlier, Sergei Rudenko had discovered the only tattooed Pazyryk ever found. Polosmak could now claim the second.[1]

On the second day, they discovered that the corpse wore a tall headdress. It was so tall it took up almost a third of the coffin. A curved wooden frame made up the inside of the headdress, around which black felt had been molded. A hat pin, ornamented with an antlerless stag, secured the headdress to the corpse's head. Beneath the unusual headpiece lay a puddle of black dye. Carved wooden swans and seven panthers adorned the vertical surface of the elaborate construction. At its base sat a mythical beast, called a griffin—half eagle, half lion. Thin sheets of gold had once covered the figures, but now much of it lay in glittering pieces inside the coffin.[2]

As soon as they found the headdress, the archaeologists knew the body was that of a woman, the first female Pazyryk discovered in a single burial. They named her Ledi, the Russian word for lady. Ledi lay on her right side with her hands folded peacefully in front of her. When the archaeologists removed the rest of the fur covering, they could see that not all of her skin survived. But her burial costume had. The archaeologists used their fingers to work away the ice around her

An intricately carved wooden griffin was one of the items found in the coffin.

clothing. As they did, it became more and more pliant. Ledi seemed to be coming to life beneath their hands.

The ancient woman wore a long woolen skirt striped with horizontal bands of white and maroon. A braided and tasseled cord encircled her waist. At her neck, she wore a string of wooden camels. Maroon piping bordered the edges of her yellow silk blouse. Around her wrist she wore a string of beads, and in her left ear, a gold earring. More tattoos adorned her wrist and thumb. Why the Pazyryk tied two pieces of string around Ledi's fingers remains a mystery.[3]

A Troubling Question

Despite their excitement at her discovery, the archaeologists became more and more uncomfortable as Ledi emerged from the ice. They knew that when the Pazyryk buried her, they expected Ledi to sleep peacefully in her kurgan forever. Now, more than 2,000 years later, archaeologists were about to yank her from her place of rest to be studied, poked, and prodded. Some of the workers began having nightmares, and rumors circulated. Some felt the gods were telling them to stop the excavation.

Whether or not to excavate a body is a question that plagues archaeologists and others. It's not easy to justify removing one from its burial place. Many people object to the practice. An example of this is the Native American population in the United States and Canada. For years, museums in these countries have sponsored archaeological expeditions to retrieve native bodies from their ancient burial grounds. Afterward, they display the remains in their museums. Native American leaders have asked that this practice be stopped and that their ancestors be returned to sacred ground.

Though digging up Ledi made the team uneasy, it didn't stop them. They decided that Ledi could act as a time-traveling ambassador and teach the modern world about her ancient one. Later, they reasoned, she could be reburied in her kurgan. First, they needed to get Ledi back to civilization. For almost two weeks after they pulled her from the grave, archaeologists continued excavating her tomb. Meanwhile, Ledi lay covered with a thin sheet of gauze on a plywood board in one of the huts. To keep her body from drying out, archaeologists sprayed water on it. It was a temporary measure and not a very good one. Once she was out of her frozen tomb, mold began to grow on her body. Archaeologists knew that to prevent further decay, they would soon need to transport the body to a freezer.[4]

Once Ledi was removed from the ice that had preserved her for so many years, the mummy began to decay.

DISASTER THREATENS

It wasn't until they tried to remove Ledi from the Ukok that bad luck descended. An early snowstorm struck on the day the helicopter was due to arrive to take them away. It was August 2. Snow fell for three days, and the helicopter arrived five days later than scheduled, on August 7. By this time, the archaeologists had already refilled most of the kurgan and had broken camp. They were ready to go home.

After they loaded their gear and Ledi into the helicopter, the team finally relaxed, relieved that their journey was almost over. Then, about 90 miles from Novosibirsk, one of the engines suddenly gave out, leaving the machine spinning dangerously at 3,000 feet above the ground. The pilot managed to safely land the helicopter in a farmer's field. Within hours, a truck arrived to take the crew and Ledi to Novosibirsk.[5]

Hidden Surprises

Back at the laboratory, archaeologists stored Ledi in an old cheese freezer. Natalya Polosmak contacted Rudolph Hauri, a forensic pathologist who works for the Swiss police. Hauri examines the bodies of murder victims, looking for clues that will tell police how they died and who killed them. Polosmak knew Hauri could apply those same skills to this case.

X-ray examinations clearly showed the sutures of Ledi's skull, the places where the plates of the skull join together. In very young babies, these plates are spaced slightly apart to accommodate the child's growing brain. As human beings mature to full size, their brains stop growing. That's when the sutures of the skull begin to fuse, or join together. Hauri could tell from Ledi's sutures that she was about twenty-five years old when she died.[6]

> The cheese freezer where Ledi was being stored malfunctioned shortly after she got there. Mold started growing again on her body, and the tattoos were beginning to fade. The archaeologists sent Ledi to Moscow for a chemical bath. The chemicals used in this bath are the same ones used to preserve the bodies of former Communist leaders, like Vladimir Lenin.

The X rays of Ledi's body showed no obvious cause of death. But as Hauri studied the body, he saw a 1.6-inch hole in the back of her skull. At first, Hauri thought this hole may have been the cause of Ledi's death, but then he looked closer. The pathologist knew that living bone is very flexible. Dead bone, on the other hand, is brittle. By studying the fractures around it, Hauri could see the hole in Ledi's skull bore marks of brittle bone. The hole came after Ledi died.

What could this mean? As Hauri continued his investigation, he soon found out. Probing Ledi's brain case with his forceps, he discovered Ledi's skull held something other than her brain. The Pazyryk had removed it and then stuffed the woman's head with fur from a pine marten, a relative of the weasel. They didn't stop there. As Hauri investigated further, he found incisions on Ledi's body. To complete the embalming process, the Pazyryk had removed all of the ancient woman's organs and then sewed her up with braided horsehair thread. They had even taken away her womb, which would have told scientists if Ledi ever had children. In place of her organs, the Pazyryk stuffed Ledi's body with peat moss and bark. Both contain tannin, a preservative that kept her body from decomposing totally.[7]

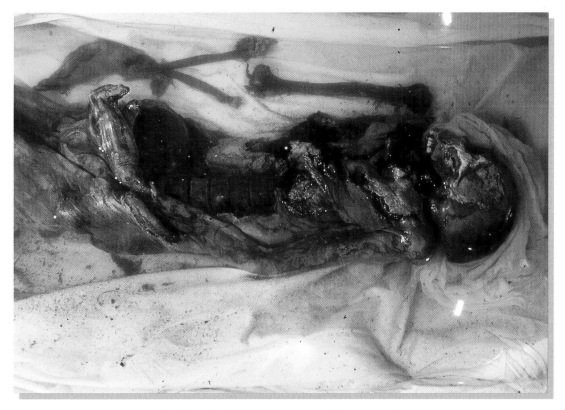

*Archaeologists in Moscow used a preserving
solution to prevent further decay.*

Preserving the Dead

When a body dies, decay begins. Modern science has helped us understand that decay begins in the gut. There, microorganisms, which once helped the body digest its food, begin to digest the body instead, in a process called autolysis. Veins and arteries serve as corridors for the organisms to move through the body. As they do, the body swells and bloats, up to three times its normal size, with the waste materials left behind by the organisms. This swelling puts pressure on the lungs, which in turn pushes bloody fluid from the mouth. The skin changes color as it decomposes and soon collapses as the internal organs disintegrate.

Some ancient cultures developed beliefs that made it necessary to stop these changes, and they developed an embalming process. For some, a mummified body served as a container where the dead person's spirit would live forever in the afterlife. By observing the way dead animals decomposed, people learned that by removing the gut, they slowed the process of decay. Many cultures refilled the body with natural substances so it would stay as true to its original shape as possible.[8]

Scientists knew the Pazyryk embalmed some of their dead. When Rudenko excavated Pazyryk kurgans earlier this century, he discovered several examples of their ancient embalming technique. In kurgan 2, both the man and woman's guts had been removed and their heads had been trepanned. Trepanning means cutting a hole in the skull. In this case, the Pazyryk used a chisel and mallet to perform the operation. After they removed the brains, the ancient embalmers replaced them with soil, pine needles, and cones from a larch tree. Afterwards, they pushed the bone back in place and sewed the skin over the hole with sinew thread. Like Ledi, their internal organs had been replaced with plant material.

Another couple in kurgan 5 were embalmed in a similar way. The Pazyryk had cut slits over the man's entire body. Scientists believe the Pazyryk placed a preservative in the slits. The preservative was probably salt, but any evidence of the substance washed away when water seeped into the tomb. The Pazyryk stripped away the muscle beneath the woman's neck and breasts and replaced it with horsehair padding.[9]

THREE

LIFE AND

DEATH

A picture of Ledi's life was beginning to form from the evidence scientists gathered. It appeared the Pazyryk considered her an important person. Like the chieftain found in kurgan 2, she bore elaborate animal tattoos on her skin. At 5 feet 6 inches, she was tall for her time and wore a very tall headdress to accentuate that height. In all the Pazyryk tombs investigated so far, the Pazyryk had reserved their most royal burials for the tallest among them. While Ledi's burial wasn't as rich as the chieftain's, it was richer than more common burials. Ledi also owned horses, regally outfitted in gilded trappings and buried alongside her tomb—a sign of her position.[1]

While it's exciting to recreate a picture of ancient life, scientists can never be sure if they're interpreting the evidence correctly. All they can do is put forth theories. That means making educated guesses about something that isn't completely proven yet. It seems clear now that Ledi's was no ordinary burial. During previous excavations, all females found in kurgans accompanied men. Because of this, some historians theorize women had a less important role in Pazyryk society. Ledi is the only exception so far, and with the discovery of this woman buried alone and so regally, historians must rethink their theories.

A ceramic dish found in the coffin next to Ledi's headdress adds to the speculation about her life. The ceramic dish contained seeds of coriander, an herb often used in modern-day cooking. In ancient times, however, people burned aromatic coriander seeds to mask unpleasant odors. Since coriander has a high ether content, they also used it for medicinal purposes. Ether is a liquid, which when burned and inhaled can be used as an anesthetic to dull pain. Polosmak believes Ledi may have been a shaman—in this case, a medicine woman who uses supernatural spirits and medicinal herbs in her work as a priestess and doctor. Polosmak believes the dish of coriander seed is symbolic of Ledi's profession.[2]

BEYOND DEATH

These remains exist because of the Pazyryk belief in the afterlife. Without the things they buried with their dead, we would have very little knowledge of their 2,500-year-old culture.

The afterlife of Ledi's possessions, as well as her spirit, interested the team excavating her tomb. Archaeologists learn about ancient cultures by studying the

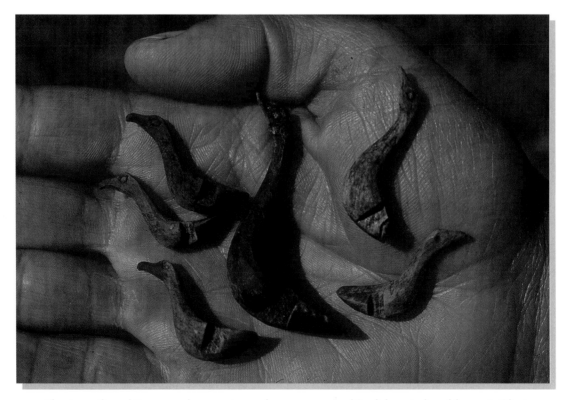

The team found tiny wooden carvings of geese near Ledi's elaborate headdress. Artifacts such as these help us to understand customs and beliefs of ancient peoples.

artifacts associated with them. For example, sometimes the symbols portrayed through a culture's art reveal more about its spiritual beliefs. The cut and weave of people's clothing can tell something about the techniques they used to make it. Knowing the materials an artifact is made from can help scientists determine if the people had trading contacts beyond their borders. And sometimes artifacts reveal close ties between an ancient culture and a modern one.

When archaeologists excavated Ledi's tomb, they found a wooden cup with two cats carved into its handle. Inside appeared to be the remains of a dairy product, either yogurt or koumiss, which is fermented mare's milk. Accompanying Ledi in her afterlife were a beautifully crafted pitcher made of animal horn and a felt saddle cover decorated with a pair of winged lions.

The Pazyryk also buried Ledi with two short-legged tables. When the archaeologists discovered them, they were frozen at the top of the burial chamber, where they had floated when the tomb first filled with water. On one of the tables, made from a birch tree, lay the remains of kurdyuk, the short fatty tail of a sheep. Modern-day residents of the Ukok eat kurdyuk, and consider it a delicacy. On the other table lay a hunk of horse meat with a bronze knife sticking into it. So well had ice preserved these things that when the meat defrosted, it started to rot and stink. Unfrozen meat would have disintegrated centuries earlier.[3]

Behind Ledi's knee lay a red cloth case. Inside the case were several beads, tiny bronze bells, and a wooden hand-mirror with a carved reindeer on its back. The mirror is one of many found in Pazyryk graves. Men, women, and even children carried them. While mirrors were a common personal possession, they may also have held magical significance for the Pazyryk. Many of the burial mirrors originated in China. Historians know from ancient writings that the Chinese considered mirrors a powerful way to ward off evil spirits. The Pazyryk may have believed the same thing. A mirror would have been an important tool for a fortune-teller, and a shaman would have used a mirror to cure illness. A Pazyryk warrior took one into battle, carrying it in a cloth bag suspended from the saddle.[4]

ELABORATE PREPARATIONS

Mirrors are just one example of Pazyryk beliefs. Another is the elaborate way they sent their loved ones to the afterlife. Evidence from the kurgan doesn't tell us how or when Ledi died, but it does tell us how and when she was buried.

Upon her death, Ledi's people set off for a forest 15 miles away to collect a larch tree with which to make her coffin. Others began digging her grave. From the kurgans Sergei Rudenko excavated, we know the Pazyryk used wooden tools such as wedges, mallets, and shovels, along with antler picks, to dig the graves, which are usually 10 feet deep and at least that wide and long.

Through the science of dendrochronology, archaeologists can learn a lot about the wooden objects in Ledi's tomb. A dendrochronologist interprets tree-ring growth patterns to determine the dates of historical and weather-related events. Every year that a tree grows, it adds another layer of plant tissue to its circumference. Weather and other factors affect the amount of plant tissue that grows in any given year. In times of drought, the rings are narrow, reflecting the hardship trees faced that growing season. In good growing years, rings are thicker. These events affect all trees the same in any particular area.

The archaeologists had to dig down 8 to 10 feet to expose the burial chamber.

For the study of Ledi's wooden grave objects, Swiss dendrochronologist Mathias Siefert used a microscope to examine core samples taken from the larch coffin and the logs of Ledi's burial tomb. By comparing the tree-ring patterns, he could tell that the logs had been harvested fifteen years before the coffin. Scientists speculate the log tomb had once been part of Ledi's house or some other construction. In tombs excavated by Rudenko, he found the same log "houses" or tombs roofed with large sheets of larch or birch bark. The bark had been boiled to make it pliable and then sewn together with twisted threads of plant fiber. The Pazyryk stuffed moss and other plants between the roof and top of the tomb to insulate the structure.[5]

FINAL FAREWELL

Those who buried Ledi placed felt at the bottom of her coffin and then laid her on top. Like all Pazyryk burials, her head lies to the east, her feet to the west. The directions east and west were significant to many ancient cultures, which associate the two directions with life and death, west being the entryway to the next world. Everything about the burial served to reflect Ledi's life in the real world. A meal of horse meat and mutton awaited her. Her most precious possessions filled her "home": the mirror, beads and bells, the horn pitcher, the tables with their dish-like tops. Six horses waited outside.

It is likely the mourners shared a last meal with Ledi. Sitting on the ground around her tomb, they probably sang songs and talked about her life. When the days of mourning ended, they refilled the hole with dirt. Next they traveled long distances to retrieve river rocks and other large stones. It probably took days, or possibly weeks, for the Pazyryk to heap stones on top of Ledi's grave.[6]

From excavations conducted by archaeologists throughout this last century, we know that Pazyryk burial procedures were very similar, but not identical. The Pazyryk covered Ledi's tomb with dirt and rocks. In the kurgans excavated by Sergei Rudenko they also used logs, mostly those of uprooted trees. All the trees were placed with their roots pointing west. The Pazyryk used an incredible number of logs. In kurgan 1, Rudenko found 300 logs. Kurgan 2 contained 240. The Pazyryk didn't stop there. In kurgan 5, they placed three layers of logs and then covered them with sixty stones. Over the horse burials in this tomb, the Pazyryk placed two boulders. One weighed 2.8 tons, the other 3.2 tons. Scientists still don't know how they moved such large boulders to the burial site.

From other evidence within the tombs, scientists know the seasons the Pazyryk usually laid their dead to rest, though they can't determine the exact year. Given the cold climate of Siberia, it makes sense that burials would have taken place when the ground was unfrozen, during the very short season between May and August. Evidence Rudenko discovered confirms this. Within the roofing insulation of kurgan 3, he found the flowers of two plants that bloom only at the end of June and very early July.[7]

The horses buried in the kurgans give scientists another clock by which to judge time. The horses in Rudenko's kurgans were very thin, as they would be after a long winter on the Ukok Plateau. But they weren't killed in winter. Their coats were thin, warm-weather coats.

The horses in Ledi's tomb gave an even more accurate timing for the burial. By examining the horses' stomachs and intestines, also called the gut, scientists can

Horses, which were valued possessions of the Pazyryk, were often buried with their owner. Shown here is the skull of one of the horses buried with Ledi.

pinpoint almost to the week when Ledi was laid in the ground. The horses' guts show that birch twigs were part of the animals' last meal. Buds had just started to form on the twigs, which means the buds were eaten sometime in June. Also, scientists found larvae of a parasitic horsefly called *gastrophilus intestinitus*. This par-

The Pazyryk buried their dead in good weather, but it's a fair guess that not all their people waited until summer to die. The Pazyryk probably stored the bodies someplace until the weather turned warm. Embalming would have kept the corpse well preserved until then.

ticular fly lays its eggs on the skin of the horse, which then licks them off. The larvae then develop in the horse's intestines. Scientists know the larvae remain in the gut only during the last two weeks of June, which is when Ledi's horses died.[8]

FOUR

HORSE

POWERED

Ledi and her people considered horses indispensable. They counted on them for everything. They consumed their flesh, drank their milk, made straps and containers from their skin, used their hair as thread, and rode them far and wide. And when it was time for their owner to pass from this life to the next, horses went along.

To prepare for their deaths, Ledi's horses were led to the ancient woman's graveside. The Pazyryk likely blindfolded the animals to calm them. Then, one by one, they were sacrificed. A swift, sure blow to the forehead with a chekan, or battle ax, usually did the job. But some of Ledi's horses were strong enough to survive that first blow. Archaeologists found two holes in some horses' heads, which means the executioner needed a second blow to complete the job. After they killed the animals, the Pazyryk lowered them into the burial chamber with ropes, taking care to fold the horses' legs beneath them. Like all Pazyryk kurgans, the horses rested in the northernmost third of the burial chamber, their heads pointing to the east. The Pazyryk were possessive about their horses. Sending their favorite animals to the afterlife in this way also meant that no one else would ever ride them.

Ledi's horses went to their deaths wearing beautiful trappings, called caparisons. The first to die wore golden griffins emblazoned on its bridle. Carved

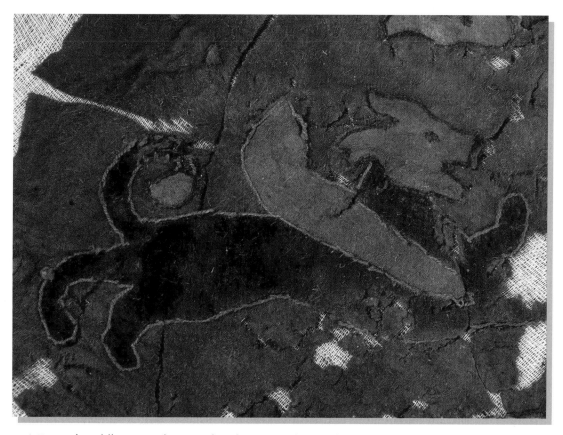

A Pazyryk saddle cover decorated with a winged animal. Today, people who live in the same region still place great value on their horses and decorate their bridles and saddle covers.

rams, covered with gold foil, adorned another. All the horses wore equally beautiful bridles and breast straps. Large felt fish dangled from saddle covers draped over their backs. The Pazyryk also braided and festooned the horses' tails.[1]

MODERN HORSE RIDERS

Investigating burial goods is just one method scientists and historians use to learn how the Pazyryk related to their horses. Another method uses ethnographic accounts. Ethnography is the branch of anthropology that records the customs and beliefs of individual cultures. In the case of the Pazyryk, ethnographers look at modern-day residents of the Altai Mountains because they believe today's Altaians share many customs with the ancient equestrians.

Ethnographers began studying modern Altaians in the nineteenth century. Sergei Rudenko, the most famous of the kurgan archaeologists, was an ethnographer, too. Much of the information we have about Altaian culture we know from his work in the region.

Rudenko found that Altaians love their horses as much as the Pazyryk did. Some families possess herds that number in the hundreds and even in the thousands. Like the Pazyryk, Altaians drink koumiss. During times in their history, Altaians considered a horse to be the only thing as valuable as a human life. Nineteenth-century Altaians could use horses to pay fines for murder or other crimes. A woman who had many horses in her kalym, or dowry, was considered a good prospect for marriage. A dowry is a gift of money or other things that a woman brings to her husband upon their marriage.[2]

Ethnographers find traces of ancient Pazyryk burial practices among Altaians. Until the end of the nineteenth century, a group called the Telesi buried horses with their owner. There is evidence that other groups, the Kazakhs and Kirgiz, once buried horses, too—until their Islamic religion discouraged it.

A remnant of the custom remained until the mid-nineteenth century. When a rich Kazakh or Kirgiz died, mourners assembled for a great feast. During the feast, the man's family brought out his favorite riding horse and turned its saddle upside down on the animal's back. Then they laid his clothing on top of the saddle and led the horse to the man's tent. As the mourners sang, someone cut the horse's tail. From then on, everyone referred to that horse as a widow, and it was never ridden again.[3]

FUN IN THE SADDLE

Ethnographers find more than just gloomy burial practices when they visit the Altai. It's hard to spend all day in the saddle without ever thinking of having fun. And like most people, Altaians like nothing more. If you visit the Altai today, you might see some of the games they play on their horses. One is Kokpar. For Kokpar, players use a headless goat carcass as a "ball." To score points, players must scoop up the goat as they ride by and carry it past the goal post. The game is played with lots of fast riding, accompanied by raucous whooping from the players. The riders aren't the only ones who get excited about the game. The horses do, too.

Another game is Kizkool, or Kiss the Girl. Players in this game are young couples about to marry. In the first half of the game, the woman gets a head start, racing her horse to reach the finish line before her future husband catches up. All the while, he's pressing his horse to go as fast as it can. When he reaches her, the man pulls her close and plants a kiss on her mouth. All this happens at full gallop. If he's successful, it means he'll be the boss in his new family.

The woman gets her turn, too. When she gets to do the chasing, the woman races to catch her man. If she can strike him with her horse whip before he reaches the goal, it means she'll be the boss. We don't know if the ancient Pazyryk played these exact games, but it's likely they had as much fun on their horses as modern equestrians do today.[4]

ON THE HOOVES OF HISTORY

It is hard to believe that by taming and riding horses, early equestrians like the Pazyryk changed the world. But they did, and it was a change that was to last for almost 6,000 years, until trains, automobiles, and other mechanized transportation replaced our dependency on the swift, versatile horse. The change came

This carved wooden horse was found when archaeologists excavated another Pazyryk kurgan.

quickly. Riding horses meant that where people once moved slowly on foot for limited distances, they could now move many times faster and farther. Goods moved swiftly, too, and trade routes opened between areas that were once isolated from each other. The fact that trade routes opened up is evident in Pazyryk burial sites, which contain items from faraway China and India.

As people came in contact with others, conflicts arose, and the horse made war a much faster and deadlier endeavor. Mounted troops, called cavalry, perfected the art of attacking on horseback as they fought the enemy. The Pazyryk, like other mounted warriors, kept the manes of their horses cropped short so they wouldn't blow in the wind and interfere with shooting an arrow.

Historians credit the Pazyryk and related tribes with the invention of pants. Before then, people usually wore scanty clothing or long, flowing robes. Of course, this type of clothing was a hindrance in horse-riding; humans needed a new garment, like pants.[5]

SMALL BEGINNINGS

None of this would have been possible if humans hadn't domesticated the horse. To understand how this happened, it helps to know the short version of the horse's long history on earth. The first horses lived 58 million years ago. Scientists call this animal *Eohippus*, dawn horse. The *Eohippus* did not look like modern-day horses. The prehistoric horse was a small, timid creature no bigger than a fox. It had four toes on its front legs and three on its hind legs, which made it easy to get around on boggy ground. *Eohippus* roamed the damp, hot jungles of the Eocene epoch, feeding on leaves and other greenery.

Over millions of years, the horse slowly evolved. It grew larger. It developed teeth strong enough to chew the toughest grasses. And because the ground had gotten firmer, it needed fewer toes to get around. By 25 million years ago, its side toes no longer reached the ground. Instead, it ran in herds on its large middle toe, which had thickened and hardened. By the Pliocene epoch, nearly 10 million years ago, the horse had developed into the stunning, swift animal we know today.[6]

TAMING THE BEAST

It wasn't until about 40,000 years ago that humans and horses finally got together—for lunch. Cave paintings show that our early ancestors hunted horses, and the archaeological record confirms this. At a Cro-Magnon site in Salutre,

France, archaeologists discovered the bones of at least 10,000 horses that had been run off a cliff by early human hunters. This is similar to how native North Americans hunted herds of bison before horses were brought to their land.

In time, humans realized they could domesticate the horse, just as they had already done with cattle, sheep, and goats. Most likely the first tamed horse was a young foal, captured when its mother died. As the horse grew, ancient humans slowly trained it to carry weight on its back as a pack animal. Anyone who has trained a horse in this way knows how hard it can be. A horse bucks and kicks when weight is placed on its back, an instinct left over from the days when it was a prey animal. The bucking reflex helps a horse survive attacks by predators that jump on its back. The next logical step was for an adventurous human to put his or her weight on a horse's back.[7]

Of course, to ride a horse, early humans first needed to control it. In the earliest days, they may have used nothing more than a rope around the horse's jaw or nose. Later, riders developed bridles that held reins and a bit, the mouthpiece used to control the horse. By the time the Pazyryk were buried in their kurgans, they had developed bridles that look very similar to those used today.

A decorated bridle made of cedar and iron shows the craftsmanship of the Pazyryk.

The Pazyryk and other Scytho–Siberian tribes spent so much time on their horses that historians believe they are the origin of the Centaur in classical mythology. The Centaurs were mythical creatures, half horse, half human.

While their bridles were similar to ours, their saddles were quite different. The Pazyryk rider sat astride a saddle composed of two small padded cushions that protected the inside of the thighs. A Pazyryk secured the saddle to the horse with a strap around its belly called a girth, a breast strap, and a crupper, which went beneath the animal's tail. They rode without stirrups, tightly gripping the horse with their thighs—a difficult task in the heat of battle or when racing.[8]

FIVE

ANCIENT

LIVES

$\mathbf{I}$t seems the ancient Pazyryk disappeared completely, leaving only their horses and other burial goods to remind us of their presence. While in many ways it is scanty, the material evidence has taught us a great deal about the Pazyryk way of life. Fortunately, there is other information that adds to the picture of the elusive horse riders.

People who investigate the ancient world turn to Herodotus's nine-book *History* to learn more. The author, who came to be known as the father of history, was born in Greece and lived from about 484 B.C. to 425 B.C. As a young man, the goings-on of the world fascinated Herodotus and gave him the urge to travel. He trekked south to Egypt, Libya, and points beyond. He then journeyed northeast toward Siberia, covering thousands of miles. These treks took many years to complete. As he traveled, he studied and wrote about the customs, ways, and religions of the cultures he encountered.

For some of his accounts, Herodotus relied on stories told to him by others, though he sometimes doubted their accuracy. Herodotus, too, may have exaggerated or been mistaken about some things. This has made later historians question his accounts. In recent years, however, archaeological evidence confirms that some of what Herodotus wrote was very close to the truth. Scholars now believe, for the most part, that *History* is a fair telescope by which to view the ancient world.

As far as we know, Herodotus didn't visit the Pazyryk, but he did visit similar horse-loving people in Eurasia. He wrote mostly about a tribe called the Scythians. The Scythians, along with other tribes—such as the Sarmatians, Massagetae, Wu-huan, and Huns—make up a group called the Scytho–Siberians. Historians consider the Pazyryk to be part of this group as well.[1]

ARCHERS AND RIDERS

The Scytho–Siberians began as a scattered collection of tribes living on the Eurasian steppes, a large area of grasslands extending 3,000 miles from the Black Sea to China. Those tribes were a unified culture from 800 B.C. to 100 B.C. Herodotus wrote that Scythians were talented archers and riders, able to shoot backwards while riding a horse at full gallop. Tribe members counted their wealth in the vast herds of horses they tended. They also buried them with their dead. In one case, Herodotus tells of 400 horses that traveled to the hereafter with their wealthy Scythian master.

These Scythian ornaments for reins are made of gold and bronze. They date from the fourth century B.C.

As with the Scytho–Siberians and many other cultures, climate affected the way the Pazyryk lived. They raised herd animals because the Altai's grasslands are perfect for grazing. Unlike the Scythians, whose changing seasons caused them to be continually searching for the best grazing grounds, the Pazyryk seemed to move infrequently. *Nomad* is the word we use to describe people who move often, as the Scythians did. *Seminomadic* describes the Pazyryk. Herodotus writes that Scythians did not build settlements or towns, so it's likely the Pazyryk didn't, either. Instead, the Pazyryk probably lived in large family groups and kept in touch with other groups living nearby, as do today's inhabitants of the Altai.[2]

Chinese chroniclers wrote the following about the Scytho–Siberian tribes they visited: "The cattle eat grass and drink water; according to the season the people move from place to place; in bad times they practice on horseback with bow and arrow, and in the good times they enjoy themselves and do not care about anything.

FIERCE FIGHTERS

Herodotus depicted the Scythians as warlike. Archaeological evidence shows this was true. Scythian kurgans yield daggers, shields, antler arrowheads, iron short swords, copper daggers, and chekans, or battle-axes. The Scythians fought for good pastureland, on which their herds depended. If their herds died, they thought nothing of stealing another tribe's herd. Herodotus says the Scythians were so warlike they drank the blood of the first enemy they killed. To receive a share of the war booty collected by his tribe, a warrior had to produce the head of a dead enemy. Herodotus also tells us the Scythians turned the skulls of their dead enemies into drinking cups.

They took scalps, too. In *History*, Herodotus described the procedure a Scythian warrior followed: "He makes a groove around the head near the ears; then he holds the head in his hands and pulls off the

Archaeologists have found a number of highly decorated weapons in Scythian kurgans, such as this sword and scabbard.

skin; then he scrapes off the fat with an ox rib and works it in his hand to make it soft; now he can use it as a duster and hangs it from the bridle of the horse he rides; he is then very proud of himself." Like the Scythians, the Pazyryk also participated in bloodletting. You may recall that the Pazyryk warrior in kurgan 2 had been scalped.[3]

EVERYDAY LIFE

Though some grave goods show the Pazyryk were warriors, other burial evidence indicates most of them lived in peace. Perhaps this was because, unlike the Scythians, they had plenty of pastureland to share. The herds of different tribes probably intermingled during good grazing weather, which made earmarks necessary. Earmarks are a pattern of cuts in an animal's ears. Each family had its own earmark to signify ownership of an animal. In winter the Pazyryk kept their herds at higher elevations where sharp winds blew snow away from the grass. In summer when the grass dried out from the wind and sun, they moved to lower, greener pastures.

Archaeologists haven't found evidence of seeds or grain in their kurgans, so it appears the Pazyryk did not farm their land. This isn't too surprising because the growing season in the Altai is very short. They may have supplemented their diet of meat and dairy products with wild plants like garlic, cedar nuts, blackberries, and rose hips.[4]

The Pazyryk considered horses their most precious commodity, but they raised other animals as well: sheep, goats, cattle, and wool-coated oxen called yaks. Archaeological evidence shows that sheep were the Pazyryk's second most important herd animal. They used it for meat, skin, wool, and milk. In every grave excavated so far, from richest to poorest, archaeologists have found offerings of mutton, which is the flesh of an adult sheep. Remember that Natalya Polosmak discovered a meal of mutton in Ledi's grave.

The animals provided wool for clothing, too. Ledi's dress had been partly woven from sheep wool. Archaeologists have discovered woolen rugs and woolen clothing in every kurgan. And of course, the Pazyryk used lots of felt, the perfect material for a culture on the go. Felt is unwoven, so it requires no loom to produce it. Instead, felt-makers boil and pound woolen fibers, which causes them to mat together. The versatility of felt meant the Pazyryk could make it as thin or as thick as they needed. They used felt for their boots and stockings, for their horse's mane and saddle covers, and to use as wall hangings, which insulated their homes from strong winter winds.[5]

This Scythian felt cloth was preserved in a frozen tomb for 2,000 years. Felt was widely used for tents, boots, wall hangings, and saddle covers.

Practical Pazyryk

The Pazyryk also used felt for their tents. They constructed a cone-shaped frame from sticks and then covered it with felt or layers of bark sewn together. Modern Altaians use similar tents, called yurts. Tents weren't the Pazyryk's permanent homes. Historians believe that since they were seminomadic, the Pazyryk probably used permanent log homes in winter, similar to the log tombs buried in their kurgans.[5]

The ancient horse riders furnished their homes with low, collapsible tables with a dish-shaped top and legs that could be easily removed for travel. Like the rest of Pazyryk belongings, these tables were sometimes decorated. The Pazyryk glued fine birch bark over some of them. Others they dyed with cinnabar (mercuric sulfide), an ore that produces a rich red color. The tables were low because the Pazyryk sat cross-legged on the floor when they ate.

The Pazyryk were resourceful people. They turned everything they could into practical items. To store food, they used clay, wood, leather, and fur containers. Examples of these containers can be found in all Pazyryk kurgans. One leather pouch found with the scalped warrior in kurgan 2 contained black dye, used to color his artificial beard. Another held the remains of cheese. Some kurgans contained round-bottomed pitchers and other vessels. Until Rudenko excavated the Pazyryk kurgans, archaeologists never understood how these bottles stood upright. In kurgan 2, he unearthed felt rings stuffed with straw and felt. The Pazyryk used the rings to support the round-bottomed containers.[6]

The Shape of Society

It's only by looking carefully at the evidence that we can piece together a picture of Pazyryk society. Historians know that pastoral tribes—those that raise herds on pastureland—are often patriarchal societies. *Patriarchal* means men are leaders of the tribe and make all the decisions. In a patriarchal society, women are considered less important. We see an example of this in an account Herodotus relates in *History*. He reports that the corpse of a supreme Scythian chief was buried with his female concubine, who had been strangled.

The patriarchal tradition doesn't apply to all the Scytho–Siberian tribes. Several of them considered women equal to men. Chinese chroniclers wrote that the Wu-huan on every matter "consult the women, who sometimes even make decisions on matters of war." Herodotus reported that in the tribe called Saromatae, "the women ride hunting and to war with the men and they dress in just the same way as the men."

Scytho–Siberian history and legends recount the stories of women taking the lead. In one, Sparetra, wife of a Sacae leader, raised an army of 300,000 men and 200,000 women when her husband was captured by the Persian king Cyrus. Her army went on to defeat him.

Rich or poor, the Pazyryk all owned personal property, which isn't the case in every culture, where sometimes only the highest rulers could possess personal property. Even the poorest burials yield grave goods and horses. Archaeologists believe the richest burials represent those of chiefs. To bury someone in such a large, elaborately prepared kurgan would have taken more than just the man's family. It would have taken an entire tribe.[7]

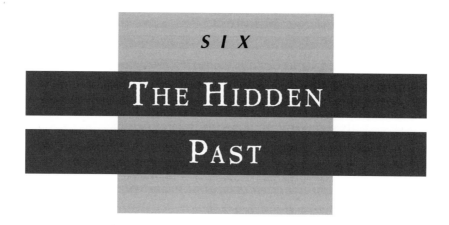

SIX

THE HIDDEN

PAST

Ledi lived in a place as far away in time as we can imagine. Fortunately, we can picture what she and her people were like. Grave goods tell us something about their funerary customs and a bit about their everyday lives. Historical accounts tell us what others saw when they visited Scytho–Siberian tribes. Ethnography helps us understand how the Pazyryk might look and act today.

However, while these things are helpful, they can't tell us what the Pazyryk were thinking. Burial items reveal little more than what they considered important for their life after death. Foreign historians reported on events and practices they may have misunderstood. Ethnography is a faint echo of past lives. If we could bring Ledi to life, she would tell us what she thought and felt about the world she lived in. But that will never happen, and the Pazyryk left no written language to tell us more. To understand the ancient equestrians, historians must rely on their interpretation of things the Pazyryk left behind.

PASSIONATE ARTISTS

Fortunately for us, the Pazyryk were passionate artists, and they left their mark on practically everything they touched. Even the most commonplace items bear dazzling displays of their talent: saddles and saddle covers, bridles, whip handles, table legs, mirrors, rugs, wall hangings, coffins, containers, cups, headdresses, and clothing. Though it's likely few people ever saw Ledi's legs beneath her long skirt, she sewed animal figures onto her hip-length, white felt stockings. To accentuate the beauty of their carvings, the Pazyryk often covered them with thin sheets of gold mined from nearby mountains.[1]

A culture's art can say a lot about its beliefs. It is clear the Pazyryk considered animals an important part of their lives. Their art portrays many kinds: deer, elk, tiger, eagle, mountain ram, and wolf. Some animals lived only within the Pazyryk imagination—griffins or fantasy creatures such as an eagle-beaked deer with a striped cat's tail.

Pazyryk art is unlike anything historians have ever seen, and it shows that the ancient horse riders were keen observers of nature. Much of their art portrays deer falling under the powerful claws of a predatory cat or other animal. Beneath these predators, the deer stumble, their hindquarters twisting upward from the impact. They throw back their heads, their eyes wide with fear.[2]

> Deer were so important to the Pazyryk that their images appear everywhere. In kurgan 1 Sergei Rudenko discovered fabulous masks worn by burial horses. To these masks, the Pazyryk attached full-sized deer antlers made of felt and leather. On one, tufts of dyed-red horsehair sprout from the antler tips. At the front, the Pazyryk placed a tiger cut from dyed-blue fur. Onto this fur, they glued many golden disks.

THE ARTIST'S CANVAS

The Pazyryk also decorated their bodies. A Greek historian named Xenophon wrote that the bodies of the rich Mossynoeci, another Scytho–Siberian group, "were drawn over and the front part tattooed in colors." Ledi had tattoos on her shoulder, wrist, and thumb. The chieftain in kurgan 2 sported tattoos from shoulder to wrist and on his legs and chest. We don't know if other parts of his body bore tattoos. Some of his skin disintegrated during his long burial, and some was cut up by looters who stole the jewelry he wore.

It's hard to know exactly what these tattoos symbolize. If they represent Pazyryk stories or myths, their meaning is lost to us. The tattoos may have been purely decorative, for the Pazyryk loved to embellish every surface they could find. Perhaps the designs signify royal stature or courageous acts. Or they may be apotropaic—that is, intended to ward off evil spirits. Scientists suspect that the

Pazyryk used some tattoos as a cure. The chieftain may have believed circular tattoos along his spine helped ease back pain. Many ancient cultures used tattoos in similar ways.[3]

BODY AND SOUL

The Pazyryk may have believed that tattoos gave them special powers. Anthropologists call this belief animism. Animists are convinced that all natural objects have a soul. By tattooing themselves with a picture of an animal they admired, the Pazyryk may have felt they took the animal's soul and gained its power.

Animists think their own bodies contain a special soul, a soul whose power extends to every part of the body. If you possess a person's body parts, you possess part of that soul. Many animists save their hair and fingernail clippings for this very reason. In kurgans 1 and 2 Rudenko discovered locks of human hair sewn

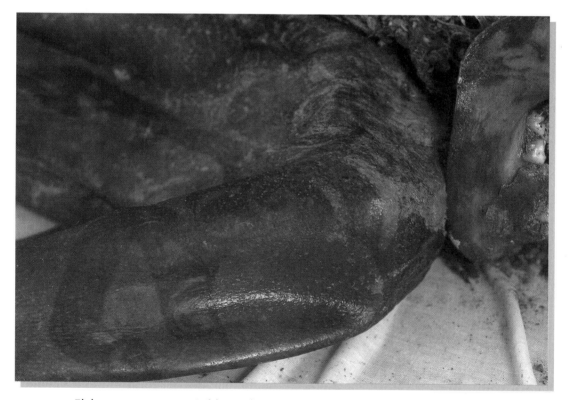

Elaborate tattoos are visible on this 3,000-year-old mummy found in Siberia. Tattooing has been practiced in various parts of the world for 10,000 years.

into pieces of leather and felt. Kurgan 2 also yielded fingernails, which were kept in a leather bag.[4]

Animism may explain another Scytho–Siberian custom related by Herodotus. The historian wrote that when an Issedones dies, "all the relatives bring cattle to his son, they kill the animals, cut up the flesh of the corpse into pieces, mix up all the meat and arrange a feast." The Massagetae did the same thing. "When someone grows old . . . they kill him and also a variety of animals, cook them up together and eat them." By eating the corpse, mourners hoped to gain some of their loved one's special powers. During embalming, the Pazyryk sometimes removed the corpse's muscles. This practice is not part of usual embalming methods of other cultures. Anthropologists speculate the Pazyryk ate the muscles of their loved ones.[5]

ANCIENT SHAVERS

It's not easy to interpret ancient clues. Hair-shaving is one example of this. In kurgan 5, Rudenko discovered a man and woman whose heads had been partially shaven. A Chinese chronicler wrote that the Wu-huan regarded it as more convenient to shave their heads. When Rudenko excavated kurgan 2, he discovered the woman's head had been completely shaven. Her locks lay beside her in the grave. Scientists suspect this particular head-shaving was in preparation for trepanation, or the removal of the woman's brain. Until archaeologists discover other clues, we may never know if head-shaving was common among the Pazyryk or if they were shaved only before burial.

Their curious hair customs extended to men's beards as well. Most Pazyryk mummies bear no evidence of beards and mustaches. The men either shaved or plucked out their beard hairs. Some men, however, wore artificial beards, attached to their face with leather straps. Archaeologists found one beneath the chieftain's head in kurgan 2. It was made of human hair dyed an intense shade of black and sewn to a strip of leather.[6]

THIEVERY!

Of course, if thieves hadn't gotten to Rudenko's kurgans first, we would know a lot more about the Pazyryk. But the looters did their job thoroughly. They began by burrowing through the center of the kurgan, throwing out cap stones and dirt as they went. When they reached the log tomb, they hacked at it with their axes.

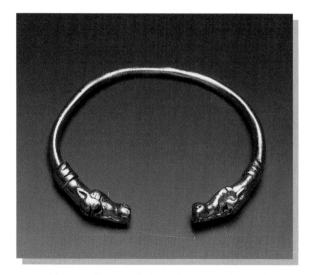
Thieves often raided tombs to steal jewelry such as this 2,000-year-old bracelet of gold.

When they encountered ice, they lit fires atop the tomb. Char marks on the logs from kurgan 2 bear witness to these fires. Archaeologists know from ax marks on the logs that looters used bronze celts, or axes. This shows they likely lived during the same time period as the Pazyryk. They may have even known the Pazyryk and looted the graves only after the equestrians had moved to their summer pastures.

Once inside, the thieves set about stealing everything they could—wall hangings, rugs, clothing, containers, and household goods. They even took arrowheads from their shafts. They threw the corpses around, and hacked off their heads to get at gold torcs they wore around their necks. They cut away feet, legs, and arms to get at gilded bracelets and anklets. The thieves used Pazyryk tabletops to carry loot from the graves and left only what they dropped or could not carry away.

Considering how much the looters left behind, we can only imagine how full of artifacts these kurgans were. Fortunately, kurgan 2 gives us a good idea. When robbers reached the chieftain's tomb, they found it locked in ice, just as Ledi's tomb was. The robbers tried chopping through it, but the ice stopped them. Until Polosmak discovered Ledi's unlooted tomb, kurgan 2 was one of the richest sources of archaeological information on the Pazyryk.[7]

POLITICAL TURMOIL

Looting a tomb is a terrible thing, yet modern Altaians think grave robbers are still at work in their land today. They believe the thieves are Russian archaeologists who come yearly to excavate kurgans on the Ukok Plateau and in other Altaian regions. They point to Ledi as an example of this thievery.

Some Altaians were horrified when archaeologists removed Ledi from her kurgan. That horror turned to outrage when they saw results of a facial reconstruction Russians completed on the ancient woman. To reconstruct a human face, a sculptor uses a base made from the mold of the skull. She then places clay over it, matching the depth of clay to certain racial characteristics. The Russian sculptor gave Ledi Caucasoid features. The Altaians, many of whom are of the Mongoloid race, disagree with the artist's interpretation. Scientists also disagree with the sculptor's interpretation and say that many of Ledi's facial characteristics show she was of the Mongoloid race. The Altaians believe the Russians made her more European-looking so they could justify keeping her body in their museum. The Altaians eventually prevailed. Ledi has come home to the mountains and now rests in an Altaian museum.[8]

The political controversy didn't stop with Ledi. In 1995 Russian archaeologists unearthed another Pazyryk mummy they dubbed the Horseman. The 2,500-year-old man wears a thick woolen cap, high leather boots, and a coat made of sheepskin and marmot, an animal related to the woodchuck. The Pazyryk buried him with his bow and arrows, an ax, and his knife. Like Ledi, his horse accompanied

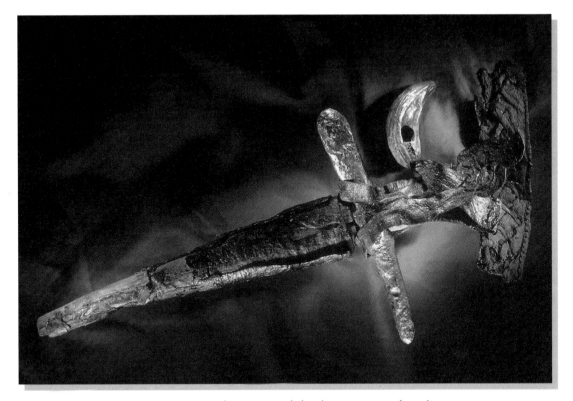

*A ceremonial iron ax with leather strap was found
in the excavation of a Pazyryk kurgan.*

him to the afterlife. It appears the Horseman died after being impaled on an enemy's weapon or by the horn of an animal. After he died, the Pazyryk embalmed him. Some of his skin survived burial, and on that skin is a deer tattoo. Officials from the Altai Republic are angry because archaeologists have taken the ancient man's body to Russia. They no longer allow Russian excavations in their country.[9]

Life After Death

Twenty-five hundred years ago, the Pazyryk carefully prepared Ledi's body for the journey to the next world. If Ledi went peacefully to her death, it's likely she had time to consider that world. Even Ledi's wildest thoughts of the future didn't include twentieth-century archaeologists, autopsies, photo shoots, and newspaper reports. Would she be upset to know her body and possessions now lie in a museum case?

We don't know the answer to this question or if we are justified in digging up ancient human remains. Perhaps all that we can do is be grateful for the chance to meet Ledi and to learn about her culture.

ANCIENT HORSEMEN

OF SIBERIA

58 MILLION YEARS AGO	*Eohippus*, dawn horse, first appears
40 MILLION YEARS AGO	*Mesohippus* develops from *Eohippus*
25 MILLION YEARS AGO	*Merychippus* develops from *Mesohippus*
10 MILLION YEARS AGO	*Pliohippus* appears, the first true monodactyl (one-toed) horse
500,000 B.C.	early humans hunt horses for food
4,000–3,000 B.C.	horse first domesticated
4,000 B.C.	first horse bridled and ridden
670 B.C.	Scythian cavalry first noted in historical records
800–100 B.C.	Pazyryk and other Scytho–Siberian cultures flourish
400 B.C.	Pazyryk erect burial kurgans 1-5

1929	kurgan 1 excavated by Sergei Rudenko
1947–1978	kurgan 2 excavated by Rudenko
1948	kurgans 3 and 4 excavated by Rudenko
1949	kurgan 5 excavated by Rudenko
1993	Ledi's kurgan excavated by Natalya Polosmak
1995	The Horseman excavated by Russian archaeologists

GLOSSARY

Altaian people who live in the Altai mountains, including Kazakhs and Kirgiz

Amazon one of a race of female warriors, reportedly belonging to a Scytho–Siberian tribe in the first century B.C.

anesthetic a drug that causes an insensitivity to pain

animism the belief that natural objects possess a soul

anthropologist a scientist who studies the cultural development, social customs, and beliefs of humans

apotropaic intended to ward off evil

archaeologist one who studies ancient people and their artifacts

bit the mouthpiece of a bridle, used to control or restrain a horse

bridle a type of head harness worn by a horse, used to control its actions

caparisons decorative covering for the harness of a horse

Caucasoid a member of a racial group with a tendency toward thin lips, a straight nose, and an iris either light or dark in color

cavalry soldiers who ride horses

celt a prehistoric ax of stone or metal

chekan battle ax

chronicler a person who records events

cinnabar mercuric sulfide, used as a dye

circumference the outer boundary, especially of a circular area

commodity something of use and value

concubine a secondary wife

core sample the central part of an object, used for examination and study

coriander a plant and herb

Cro-Magnon an upper Paleolithic race of humans, considered to be the first Europeans

croup the highest part of a horse's hindquarters

crupper a leather strap, fastened to the saddle, that loops beneath the horse's tail

dendrochronology the study of tree ring growth patterns to determine past events

dowry the goods a woman brings to a man when they marry

drought an extended period of dry weather

earmark a pattern of nicks and wedges cut into a horse's ears to indicate ownership

embalming to treat a dead body with materials that will help preserve it

Eohippus an extinct horse from the Eocene epoch; dawn horse, the first horse

equestrian a person who rides horses

ether a gaseous anesthetic

ethnography the branch of anthropology that records the customs and beliefs of individual cultures

felt a nonwoven fabric of wool, fur or hair matted together by heat, moisture and pressure

festoon to decorate with string, ribbon, or flowers

forensic pathologist a scientist who studies human bodies to determine cause of death

gastrophilus intestinitus   a parasitic horsefly

gilded   covered with gold

girth   belly strap of a saddle

griffin   an imaginary creature with the body of a lion and the head and wings of an eagle

grunt work   hard labor

gut   esophagus, stomach, intestines

hereafter   a life or existence after death

kalym   dowry

Kizkool   Altaian game played on horseback by young couples

Kokpar   Altaian game played on horseback

Kora kobinsi   a group of people who buried their dead in Pazyryk tombs

koumiss   fermented mare's milk

kurdyuk   the fatty tail part of a sheep, considered a delicacy

kurgan   burial mound

larvae   immature, wingless insects

marmot   an animal related to woodchucks

mercury sulfide   a chemical used as a red dye, cinnabar

Mongoloid   a race of humans characterized by their prominent cheekbones, straight black hair, small nose, and broad face

mutton   the meat of an adult sheep

nomad   a member of a tribe that moves frequently

pastoral   having to do with pastures

patriarchal   dominated by males

permafrost   subsoil that is always frozen

pine marten   relative of the weasel

piping   the trim on clothing

plateau   a high, flat area of land

Pliocene epoch   a period occurring from 10 million to 1 million years ago; the number of mammals increased during this time

Scytho–Siberians   a unified culture that lived on the Eurasian steppes during the first century B.C.

seminomadic   moving infrequently or seasonally

shaman   a medicine man or woman, who uses supernatural powers and herbs to treat the sick and to perform certain rites

sutures   the places where the plates of the skull meet

torc   a band of metal worn around the neck by some ancient people

trepanning   cutting a hole in the skull

womb   the female organ where babies develop

yurt   a tent used by modern Altaians

SOURCE NOTES

ONE: PASTURES OF HEAVEN

1. Natalya Polosmak, "Pastures of Heaven." *National Geographic* (October 1994): 80–99.

2. Ibid.

Jeanne Louise Smoot, personal communication. Jeanne Smoot traveled to the Altai as an undergraduate student in anthropology at Harvard University. She participated in the excavation of Ledi's kurgan.

3. Polosmak, "Pastures of Heaven," 95.

Sergei Rudenko, *Frozen Tombs of Siberia,* trans. by M. W. Thompson. (Berkeley and Los Angeles, Calif.: University of California Press, 1970): 212.

Jeanne Louise Smoot, unpublished thesis manuscript, (Cambridge: Harvard University, March 1994), 10, 58.

Esther Jacobson, *The Deer Goddess of Ancient Siberia: A Study in the Ecology of Belief,* (The Netherlands: E. J. Brill, 1993): 42.

4. Polosmak, "Pastures of Heaven," 95.

Smoot, thesis, 57–61.

Rudenko, *Frozen Tombs*, 11, 35.

5. Smoot, personal communication

6. Polosmak, "Pastures of Heaven," 96.

7. Ibid., 96.

Smoot, thesis, 46.

8. Polosmak, "Pastures of Heaven," 96.

Smoot, personal communication.

Andrew Thompson, producer, *The Ice Maiden,* BBC Horizon (documentary), January 1997.

9. Polosmak, "Pastures of Heaven," 96–97.

Smoot, personal communication.

10. Polosmak, "Pastures of Heaven," 97.

Thompson, *The Ice Maiden*.

TWO : ANCIENT ICE

1. Polosmak, "Pastures of Heaven," 95–99.

2. Ibid., 98–99.

3. Ibid., 95–99.

4. Ibid., 95–103.

Smoot, personal communication.

5. Polosmak, "Pastures of Heaven," 95–103.

Smoot, personal communication.

6. Thompson, *The Ice Maiden*.

7. Ibid.

8. Rudenko, *Frozen Tombs*, 280–281.

THREE : LIFE AND DEATH

1. Polosmak, "Pastures of Heaven," 91, 99.

Smoot, thesis, 39.

Thompson, *The Ice Maiden*.

2. Polosmak, "Pastures of Heaven," 99.

Smoot, thesis, 39.

Thompson, *The Ice Maiden*.

3. Polosmak, "Pastures of Heaven," 96–97

4. Ibid., 80–103.

Rudenko, *Frozen Tombs,* 116.

5. Thompson, *The Ice Maiden*.

Rudenko, *Frozen Tombs*, 19–20.

James Jerpersen and Jane Fitz-Randolph, *Mummies, Dinosaurs, Moon Rocks* (New York: Atheneum Books for Young Readers, 1996): 25–32.

6. Polosmak, "Pastures of Heaven," 90–103

7. Rudenko, *Frozen Tombs*,19–24.

8. Thompson, *The Ice Maiden*.

Smoot, thesis, 56–57.

FOUR : HORSE POWERED

1. Polosmak, "Pastures of Heaven," 91.

Thompson, *The Ice Maiden*.

2. Rudenko, *Frozen Tombs*, xxvi, 56, 117–119.

3. Ibid., 284.

4. David Anthony and Dorcas Brown, Institute for Ancient Equestrian Studies, www.hartwick.edu/anthropology/iaes.html

5. Rudenko, *Frozen Tombs*, xxv–xxvi.

David Anthony, Dorcas Brown, and Dimitri Y. Telegin, "The Origin of Horseback Riding," *Scientific American* (December 1991): 94–100.

———. International Museum of the Horse, Kentucky Horse Park, Lexington, Ky. www.imh.org/imh/kyhp (The Reluctant Rider).

6. ———. International Museum of the Horse, Kentucky Horse Park, Lexington, Ky. www.imh.org/imh/kyhp (The Early Horse).

7. ———. International Museum of the Horse, Kentucky Horse Park, Lexington, Ky. www.imh.org/imh/kyhp (The Reluctant Rider).

Rudenko, *Frozen Tombs*, xxv–xxvi.

Deborah M. Britt, *Horse Training Basics* (Loveland, Co.: Alpine Publications 1994): 34–36.

8. ———. International Museum of the Horse, Kentucky Horse Park, Lexington, Ky. www.imh.org/imh/kyhp (The Reluctant Rider).

Rudenko, *Frozen Tombs*, xxv–xxvi.

FIVE: ANCIENT LIVES

1. Rudenko, *Frozen Tombs*, 211.

———. "Herodotus." (Chicago: The New Encyclopedia Britannica, volume 5. 1995).

2. ———. International Museum of the Horse, Kentucky Horse Park, Lexington, Kentucky. www.imh.org/imh/kyhp

Polosmak, "Pastures of Heaven," 87–88.

Smoot, thesis, 7.

3. Rudenko, *Frozen Tombs,* 217–221.

4. Ibid., 55–59, 80, 215–220.

5. Ibid., 57–58, 86, 202.

6. Ibid., 62–71.

7. Ibid., 211–212.

SIX: THE HIDDEN PAST

1. Rudenko, *Frozen Tombs*, 229–269.

Polosmak, "Pastures of Heaven," 101.

2. Jacobson, *The Deer Goddess of Ancient Siberia*, 63.

3. Rudenko, *Frozen Tombs*, 110–114.

4. Ibid., 285–287.

5. Ibid., 285–287.

6. Ibid., 104–105.

7. Ibid., 7–12.

8. Thompson, *The Ice Maiden*.

9. ———. "Siberian Mummy Flap," *Archaeology* (January/February 1996). Newsbriefs. www.archaeology.org

FURTHER READING

Anthony, David and Dorcas Brown. Institute for Ancient Equestrian Studies. www.hartwick.edu/anthropology/iaes.html

Anthony, David, Dorcas Brown, and Dimitri Y. Telegin. "The Origin of Horseback Riding." *Scientific American* (December 1991).

Brier, Bob. *Encyclopedia of Mummies*. New York: Facts on File. 1997.

Davis-Kimball, Jeannine. "Warrior Women of the Eurasian Steppes." *Archaeology* (January/February 1997). www. archaeology.org

"Herodotus." Chicago: The New Encyclopedia Britannica, volume 5, 1995, 881–882.

International Museum of the Horse, Kentucky Horse Park, Lexington, Ky. www.imh.org/imh/kyhp

Jerpersen, James and Jane Fitz-Randolph. *Mummies, Dinosaurs, Moon Rocks*. New York: Atheneum Books for Young Readers, 1996.

Polosmak, Natalya. "Pastures of Heaven." *National Geographic* (October 1994): 80–103.

Putnam, Jim. *Mummy.* New York: Knopf Books for Young Readers, 1993.

Rudenko, Sergei. *Frozen Tombs of Siberia*. Trans. by M. W. Thompson. Berkeley and Los Angeles, Calif.: University of California Press.

"Siberian Mummy Flap." *Archaeology* (January/February 1996). Newsbriefs. www.archaeology.org

Thompson, Andrew, producer. *The Ice Maiden*. BBC Horizon (documentary). January 1997.

I N D E X

ABOUT THE AUTHOR

Janet Buell is an elementary school enrichment teacher. Her main interests are anthropology, archaeology, reading, soccer, and softball. The time she spent exploring a local bog made her want to find out more. In her research, she discovered the existence of bog bodies and other ancient humans. It soon turned into the idea for this book series. Janet was born and raised in Illinois and now lives in Goffstown, New Hampshire.